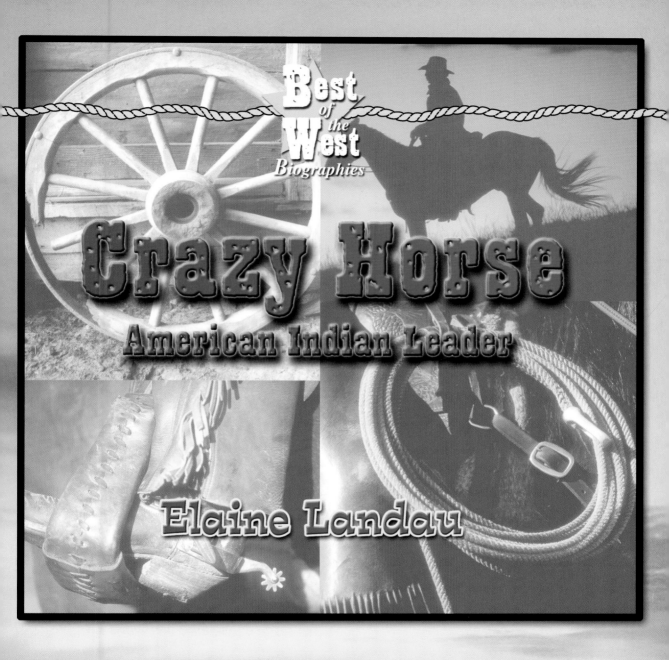

Best of the West Biographies

Crazy Horse
American Indian Leader

Elaine Landau

Enslow Publishers, Inc.

40 Industrial Road   PO Box 38
Box 398   Aldershot
Berkeley Heights, NJ 07922   Hants GU12 6BP
USA   UK
http://www.enslow.com

Editor's Note: *Crazy Horse's people called themselves the Lakota. His father was an Oglala Lakota and his mother was a Brule Lakota. The Lakota, Nakota and Dakota people are often collectively referred to as the Sioux. We at Enslow Publishers, Inc., are aware that "Sioux" is often considered as an offensive term. However, since Crazy Horse's people are still often known as the Sioux, we have decided to use this term. We mean no disrespect to the Lakota, Nakota, or Dakota people, but just wish to reach as many readers as possible in order to tell the rich history of this important leader.*

Library of Congress Cataloging-in-Publication Data

Landau, Elaine.
     Crazy Horse : American Indian leader / Elaine Landau.
          p. cm. — (Best of the West biographies)
     Summary: A simple biography of the Oglala Sioux chief who fought for the rights of Native American people and who led the defeat of General Custer at the Little Big Horn in 1876.
     Includes bibliographical references and index.
     ISBN 0-7660-2216-1 (hardcover)
     1. Crazy Horse, ca. 1842–1877—Juvenile literature.
2. Oglala Indians—Kings and rulers—Biography—Juvenile literature. 3. Dakota Indians—Wars, 1876—Juvenile literature. 4. Little Bighorn, Battle of the, Mont., 1876—Juvenile literature. [1. Crazy Horse, ca. 1842–1877. 2. Kings, queens, rulers, etc. 3. Oglala Indians—Biography. 4. Indians of North America—Great Plains—Biography.] I. Title. II. Series.
E99.O3.C7245 2004
978.004'9752—dc21

                2003010334

Printed in the United States of America

10 9 8 7 6 5 4 3 2 1

To Our Readers: We have done our best to make sure that all Internet addresses in this book were active and appropriate when we went to press. However, the author and publisher have no control over and assume no liability for the material available on those Internet sites or on other Web sites they may link to. Any comments or suggestions can be sent by e-mail to comments@enslow.com or to the address on the back cover.

Illustration Credits: © 1999 Artville, L.L.C. All rights reserved, p. 13; © Clipart.com, pp. 17, 30; © Corel Corporation, pp. 1, 2–3, 5, 12, 15, 19, 25, 26, 32, 33, 37, 42 (background); *Crazy Horse 1/34 scale model, Korczak, sculptor,* © The Crazy Horse Memorial Foundation, Photo: Robb Dewall, p. 42; John Grafton, *The American West of the Nineteenth Century* (New York, Dover Publications, Inc., 1992), pp. 10, 34; National Anthropological Archives, Smithsonian Institution/ 08583500, p. 35; Permission to use Michael Gentry art in this publication was granted by the wife of the artist, Roberta Gentry. Website for Michael Gentry art: www.michaelgentry.com, p. 4, 9; Photo Courtesy of the South Dakota State Historical Society—State Archives, pp. 29, 38; Reproduced from the Collections of the Library of Congress, pp. 20, 23, 28, 41; © Tom Ives/Corbis, p. 21; Wyoming State Archives, Dept. of State Parks and Cultural Resources, p. 7.

Cover Illustration: © Corel Corporation (Background); Permission to use Michael Gentry art in this publication was granted by the wife of the artist, Roberta Gentry. Website for Michael Gentry art: www.michaelgentry.com (Crazy Horse Portrait).

Contents

This painting by Michael Gentry is called
Crazy Horse at Rosebud.

1

A Brave Young Sioux

December 21, 1866

It was a cold winter morning. The men in the Sioux camp had been up since dawn. They were ready for action. For years, white settlers invaded the northern Great Plains. They had seized the land and killed the buffalo herds. Many Sioux had died, as well. Today, the American Indians were striking back.

They planned to raid a wagon train near Fort Phil Kearny. The fort had been built to protect the Bozeman Trail. The Bozeman was a new trail leading to Montana's gold fields. It ran straight through the Sioux's last and best hunting grounds. That threatened the survival of the American Indians.

As expected, the wagon train left the fort on time that day. Each morning, it took a group of loggers to get the fort's firewood. The American Indians watched for the wagon train from the hills. When it approached, a small band of Sioux attacked.

The frightened loggers signaled the fort for help. The soldiers there quickly came to save them. They were under the command of Captain William J. Fetterman.

Fetterman was a young officer who disliked American Indians. He had never tried to hide his feelings about them. Fetterman once had said, "Give me eighty men and I'll ride through the entire Sioux nation." On December 21, 1866, he had eighty men with him.

Fetterman wanted to fight. But the Sioux headed back toward the hills. There was no time to chase them. Suddenly, a second group of American Indians had appeared. They had been hiding in the brush near the fort. Now they were riding straight toward Fetterman.

Their leader was a young Sioux named

Captain William Fetterman did not think that American Indians were great warriors. Crazy Horse proved him wrong.

Crazy Horse. He wore a blanket around his shoulder and had a red lightening bolt painted on his cheek. Large white hail spots were painted on his body, as well.

Crazy Horse was daring. He rode within feet of Fetterman. Then, he pulled off his blanket and let out a war cry. Crazy Horse waved the blanket at Fetterman and rode off. The officer ordered his men to go after Crazy Horse. The other American Indians rode beside him. They called out to the soldiers. They dared the men to catch them.

Some of Fetterman's men were on horseback. However, others were foot soldiers. These could not keep up with the American Indians. Crazy Horse expected that, and had a plan. He wanted to stay just ahead of all the soldiers. It was important that no one fell behind. During the chase, Crazy Horse even jumped off his war pony. He looked carefully at the animal's foot. Crazy Horse hoped that the soldiers would think it had gone lame.

After that, Crazy Horse ran alongside his horse. His men surrounded him to shield him from the soldiers' bullets. Before long, the soldiers began to gain on them. Now Crazy Horse jumped back on his horse. The American Indians galloped off. They knew that the soldiers would follow. By then, Fetterman and his men were in hot pursuit.

Crazy Horse had tricked Fetterman. He and his men were not alone. They were merely decoys. They were supposed to get the soldiers to go over Lodge Pole Ridge. A large force of

American Indian fighters awaited Captain Fetterman there.

Soldiers had been led into American Indian ambushes before. The results were usually disastrous. Earlier, Fetterman had been ordered

This painting, called *Crazy Horse: Sacred Warrior*, was painted by Michael Gentry. The artist was part American Indian himself.

not to chase the American Indians too far. The officer who was his boss told him to only "support the wagons."

But Fetterman could not resist. Feeling certain of victory, he did not follow orders. Fetterman had eighty men and thought that Crazy Horse only had about ten. He told his soldiers to continue after the American Indians. They followed Crazy Horse over the ridge.

At Fort Phil Kearny, Crazy Horse and his men defeated the soldiers defending the fort.

At that point, everything changed. Fetterman's eighty soldiers now faced about two thousand American Indian warriors. Most were Sioux but others were there, too. The soldiers were stunned.

Hundreds of arrows flew quickly through the air. Large numbers of white soldiers began to fall. Many died before they could fire their guns. In under an hour, it was over. Not a single soldier was left alive.

It was an important victory for the Sioux. Much of the credit went to Crazy Horse. His skill and daring made the ambush a success. That was not the last time Crazy Horse helped his people. He would become a great Sioux leader. This is his story.

2

Growing Up Sioux

No one is sure exactly when Crazy Horse was born. But most people think it was probably in 1841. Crazy Horse was a Sioux. The Sioux nation was made up of three different groups: the Lakota, Nakota, and Dakota. Each of these three groups were divided into even more groups. Crazy Horse's father was an Oglala Lakota. His mother was a Brule Lakota. The Sioux were a proud and independent people. Before the white settlers arrived, they had never been conquered.

During his early years, Crazy Horse and his people lived on the northern Great Plains. Sioux territory was vast. It included much of what is known today as the states of Montana,

Nebraska, Wyoming, and North and South Dakota. Bands of Sioux followed the buffalo herds roaming the plains.

Crazy Horse's father was a holy man. Unfortunately, Crazy Horse's mother died when he was quite young. So the boy's aunt helped to

The Sioux were a nomadic people, which means they moved from place to place. They followed the buffalo herds through the present-day states of Nebraska, Wyoming, Montana, and North and South Dakota.

raise him, along with his older sister and younger brother.

Crazy Horse did not look like other Sioux children. He had a slender, narrow face and light skin. His hair was brown and wavy. When he was young, people called him "Curly." White people who saw him thought that he might be a white child who had been captured by American Indians. The boy was different in another way, too. He was unusually thoughtful and quiet. Unlike most young boys, Curly listened more than he spoke.

As a youth, Curly was close to his father. His father taught him the ways of their people. Curly learned to swiftly shoot a bow and arrow. He became an expert horseman and hunter. The boy killed his first buffalo when he was just ten or eleven.

These were mostly happy years for Curly. Yet even then, he knew that things were changing. Curly often watched the settlers' wagon trains from a distance. He saw that more white people were coming. He also soon

Many buffalo once roamed across America. The Sioux hunted the animals for food and to use their hides to make clothes and other items.

learned that many whites did not like or respect American Indians. Often, when white people and American Indians were together, there was bloodshed. Curly felt for his people. Yet as a boy, there was little he could do.

Before becoming a man, a Sioux boy went on a vision quest. He would go to a deserted place by himself. The boy would wait there for the sacred powers to send him a vision. That vision would help guide and protect him in life.

A vision quest was not taken lightly. A boy prepared for it for a long time. In most cases, a holy man helped him get ready.

When Curly was about thirteen, he went on a vision quest. But he did not prepare for it. Instead, Curly rode to a hilltop where he sat alone for over two days. During this time, he did not eat or sleep.

By then, Curly was ready to leave. He had not received a vision and was disappointed. He was about to mount his horse when it happened. First, Curly felt weak and dizzy. Then, he looked straight ahead and the vision appeared to him.

In his vision, Curly saw a man on a horse. The man was not wearing a war bonnet. There was just a single hawk feather in his hair. A small stone was tied behind his ear.

The horseman spoke to Curly. He told the boy how to prepare for battle. He said that

The buffalo hunt was part of life for the Sioux.

Curly should never wear a war bonnet or paint his horse. Instead, he told Curly to put some dust on the horse and on his body and hair. The horseman further warned Curly never to take anything from a defeated enemy.

In the vision, Curly saw arrows and bullets

hit the rider. Yet the man remained unharmed. The horseman also seemed to ride through a bad storm. Once again, he was not hurt. However, large, white hail spots appeared on his body. There was also a small lightening bolt on his cheek.

Curly later told his father what he saw. At first, his father was angry. He had wanted his son to properly prepare for his vision quest. But he still knew that Curly's vision was important. His father told Curly to dress like the rider before going into battle. He also told him to always do as the rider said. That way, his enemy's arrows and bullets would never do him any harm.

3

From Boy to Man

As Curly grew older, he often saw his people suffer. In the summer of 1855, he visited his Brule relatives at their camp. One morning, he left the camp to chase a wild horse. When he returned, he could not believe his eyes.

White soldiers had attacked. They had turned the camp into a field of dead bodies. Men, women, and children had been blown apart by cannon fire. Their teepees, or the tents that were their homes, were burned to the ground. Now Curly knew firsthand what the white people could do.

Curly was still too young to fight his people's enemies. He did not go out with a war party until he was seventeen. Then, he and

The Sioux often set up their teepees in the shape of a crescent moon.

some others raided an Arapaho Indian village. The Arapahos had some horses they wanted. Curly fought bravely that day. When it was over, the Sioux took the animals to their camp.

That night they had a victory celebration. In the past, Curly's father had gone by the name Crazy Horse. But to honor his son's bravery, he gave Curly his name. After that,

Curly was called Crazy Horse. His father was known as Worm.

Young Crazy Horse took part in a number of raids against different American Indian groups. He usually led the war parties. Other young Sioux admired Crazy Horse and wanted to be like him.

Crazy Horse was more than a good fighter. He was also an outstanding hunter who often led buffalo hunts. Sometimes, Crazy Horse hunted alone. He would bring back deer, elk, and geese. Crazy Horse gave much of what he caught to others. He helped feed widows and those who were too old to hunt. Crazy Horse soon became known for his kindness. People told

This Sioux dancer is ready to take part in an important ritual.

stories praising him. Yet Crazy Horse was not known to brag. He simply did what he believed was right.

But things did not always go his way. When Crazy Horse was about twenty years old, he fell in love with Black Buffalo Woman. Her uncle was Red Cloud, a rising leader among the Sioux. Crazy Horse wanted to marry Black Buffalo Woman. Unfortunately, many other young men hoped to do the same.

During the summer of 1862, Red Cloud led a Sioux raid against the Crow Indians. He took Crazy Horse along with him. The war party was gone for two weeks. By the time they returned, Black Buffalo Woman had married a man named No Water.

Some said that Red Cloud tricked Crazy Horse. They claimed that Red Cloud wanted to get Crazy Horse away from camp. That way, his niece could marry a young man from a rich and important Sioux family. Red Cloud felt that No Water's family was better than Crazy Horse's family.

No Water married the woman whom Crazy Horse loved.

Crazy Horse was very upset. His war party had been victorious. Yet he did not celebrate with the others. Instead, Crazy Horse returned to his parents' lodge. He felt no joy.

Other sorrows followed. On November 29, 1864, white soldiers attacked a Cheyenne village. Over one hundred American Indian men, women, and children were killed. The soldiers were brutal. They showed no mercy to even the youngest victims.

News of the slaughter quickly spread among the Plains Indians. They knew that there was strength in numbers. Some of the groups banded together to fight back. The Sioux were among them.

War parties were formed. By 1865, a number of raids were conducted. Crazy Horse took part in some of these raids. He often acted as a decoy. In July 1865, he lured the 11th Cavalry, a group of white soldiers, into an ambush over the Platte Bridge Station. Fooled by Crazy Horse, the soldiers had no chance to escape.

Following Platte Bridge, Crazy Horse was honored by his tribe's elders. He was made a "shirt wearer." Crazy Horse was given a special sheepskin shirt. It had 240 locks of hair sewn on it. Each lock stood for one of Crazy Horse's brave deeds.

As a "shirt wearer" Crazy Horse took on a special role. He was to help keep peace and harmony among his people. Crazy Horse was now looked upon as a leader. This was both an honor and a responsibility.

4

Victories and Defeats

Crazy Horse enjoyed a number of victories. These included the December 1866 wagon train ambush near Fort Phil Kearny. The American Indian raids along the Bozeman Trail continued. The white soldiers soon found it too difficult to defend the trail. They abandoned the forts there. In the summer of 1868, the soldiers packed up and left.

The American Indians let the white soldiers leave in peace. The next day, Crazy Horse led a group of Sioux through Fort Phil Kearny. They set fire to all the buildings. The American Indians did the same at the other Bozeman Trail forts. They wanted to make sure that the soldiers had nothing to come back to.

In 1868, Red Cloud and other Sioux leaders signed a peace treaty at Fort Laramie. It gave the American Indians nearly all of the Dakota Territory. The Black Hills were promised to the Sioux for "as long as the grass shall grow and the waters shall flow." The American Indians hoped that things would be better.

But in some ways things were not better for

After winning a battle, American Indians would often celebrate. This painting by Frederic Remington is called "Victory Dance."

Crazy Horse. He had never forgotten Red Cloud's niece, Black Buffalo Woman. Despite her marriage to No Water, Crazy Horse still loved her. In 1871, she agreed to leave her husband and ride off with Crazy Horse. No Water was furious and went after them. He found the couple a few days later. No Water shot Crazy Horse in the face. He left him for dead. Black Buffalo Woman returned to camp with No Water.

As it turned out, Crazy Horse had only been wounded. He made his way back to the camp, where his family nursed him back to health. But Crazy Horse could no longer be a "shirt-wearer." He had caused trouble among his people.

Crazy Horse finally accepted that he would never be with Black Buffalo Woman. In 1872, he married a woman called Black Shawl. The next year, the couple had a daughter. Crazy Horse named the baby They-Are-Afraid-Of-Her. He adored the little girl but their time together was short. While she was still quite young, the child died of cholera. Crazy Horse felt as if a part of him died, too. Now he spent even more time by himself.

Things became harder for the Sioux, as well. Their fight with the white soldiers was hardly over. Good hunting grounds had been promised to them. However, the white people often broke treaties. In 1873, they decided to run the Northern Pacific Railroad through Sioux territory. A group of land surveyors were sent to determine the railroad's exact route. The surveyors did not come alone. Lieutenant Colonel George Armstrong Custer and his men

George A. Custer was looking for glory when he went after the Sioux.

Sitting Bull was a Sioux leader and medicine man.

were sent to protect them from harm.

Crazy Horse wanted to stop the whites. He and another well-known Sioux leader, Sitting Bull, decided to fight them. They began a series of small raids in 1873. For a time, the surveyors left. But they came back the next year. Custer and his men returned with them. This time, Custer explored the Black Hills. He quickly announced that gold was there. Soon, large numbers of miners poured into the region. The clash between the American Indians and the white people became even worse.

In 1875, the government said that it wanted to buy the Black Hills. But this was sacred ground to the Sioux. They would not sell. The white people did not respect the beliefs of the American Indians. That same year, the government declared that all the Sioux had to live on a reservation. This was a separate area of land set aside for American Indians by the government. The Sioux had to be there by

Custer and his men rode to confront the local American Indians.

January 31, 1876. Anyone who did not go would be considered an enemy.

Crazy Horse refused to obey. He and his people joined with Sitting Bull once again. Other bands of Sioux came, too. By June 1876, 10,000 American Indians had come together to fight the white people.

The whole group set up camp in the valley of the Little Bighorn. Crazy Horse asked the Cheyenne and Blackfoot Indians to join them, as well. Everyone was prepared to fight for their freedom.

In a vision, Sitting Bull had seen many white soldiers falling into their camp. He believed that meant an American Indian victory. Yet they still had to be prepared. The American Indians sent out scouts to watch for the whites. On June 25, they spotted a group of soldiers traveling along the Little Bighorn River. They were headed straight for the American Indians' camp.

5

The Battle of the Little Bighorn

The American Indians had seen Lieutenant Colonel George Armstrong Custer leading the 7th Cavalry that day. Custer was a known hater of American Indians. Some say he was desperate for glory. But he was also impatient and sometimes took foolish risks.

Custer had been ordered not to attack if he found the American Indian camp. He was to wait for more soldiers to arrive. But Custer had other ideas. He wanted this victory badly. He thought it would help his career.

Custer divided the 7th Cavalry into three separate divisions. The first group would be led by Major Marcus A. Reno. It was to attack the American Indian camp from the south. The second was under Captain Frederick Benteen. His men would scout the surrounding area. They were to spot and stop any American Indians from escaping.

Custer led the third division. He planned to enter the American Indian camp from the north. His men would travel along a steep ridge and down a ravine to the river below. After crossing the river, they would be in the northern half of the camp.

American Indian scouts followed the movements of Custer's men.

The Sioux performed a ritual called a ghost dance before the Battle of the Little Bighorn.

At about 3:00 P.M., Major Reno and his men struck. They rode into the south end of the camp but did not get very far. The American Indians were ready for them. They fought back hard. In less than twenty minutes, many of Reno's men were down. Some had been killed. Others were too badly injured to go on fighting. Reno's group retreated.

No one is certain of Crazy Horse's role in

that part of the battle. Some say that he quickly headed for that end of the camp. They claim that he got there in time to help defeat Reno's men.

Others say that Crazy Horse arrived just as the soldiers retreated. He then headed north to cut off Custer's group. But first he rode through the village gathering men who had not yet fought. They made sure that Custer never

This pictograph by Red Horse shows the Battle of the Little Bighorn. Red Horse was an American Indian who took part in the battle.

reached the camp. Crazy Horse and his men attacked the white soldiers before they could cross the river.

Crazy Horse's group flanked the soldiers from the north and west. Other American Indians charged from the south and east. Many carried the rifles they had taken from Reno's dead soldiers. There was no way out for Custer. The soldiers were surrounded.

When it was over, George Armstrong Custer and his men were dead. The Battle of Little Big Horn was a tremendous American Indian victory. Crazy Horse had shown himself to be an outstanding leader.

After the battle, the American Indian groups split up. They knew that more soldiers would soon be there. It was too dangerous to stay at the large camp.

Crazy Horse headed southeast with about six hundred of his people. He had tasted victory, but the thrill did not last. The white soldiers kept coming.

6

The End Nears

Crazy Horse went on fighting the white people, but his raids were smaller now. He struck the miners in the Black Hills. Sometimes, he even attacked these men alone.

In December 1876, an army officer named Colonel Nelson Miles contacted Crazy Horse. Miles expected Crazy Horse to surrender. There had been several blizzards and because of the weather, game was scarce. Miles knew that made it harder for the proud American Indian leader to hold out. Crazy Horse agreed to hear what Miles had to say. He sent eight men to meet with the Colonel. But things did not go as expected. As the American Indians neared the fort, Nelson's scouts fired on them. Only three of Crazy Horse's men survived. Any hope of a peaceful surrender was over.

Colonel Miles was not about to give up. He tried to take Crazy Horse by force. He found the brave leader's camp in early January 1877. But Crazy Horse fought instead of surrendering. The fighting lasted for over seven days. It snowed heavily during that time. In the end, Miles left with his soldiers.

Yet things grew worse for Crazy Horse and his people daily. Most days the temperature dipped below zero. The American Indians were cold and hungry. Their clothes were ragged. They wondered if they

Colonel Miles would go on to defeat the Apache. However, he could not win a battle against Crazy Horse.

could defeat soldiers who were well fed and warmly dressed.

In February 1877, another white officer sent a message to Crazy Horse. He was General George Crook. Crook urged Crazy Horse to come to Fort Robinson, Nebraska, to surrender. He said that Crazy Horse could have his own reservation in the Powder River area. The Sioux had often hunted buffalo there.

By then Crazy Horse knew that he could no longer fight the white people. He agreed to surrender at the fort. He and about a thousand of his people arrived there in May 1877. They gave up their weapons. Crazy Horse and his people were anxious to leave for their own reservation. However, they never got their own land. It was just another broken promise.

Crazy Horse lived in a lodge near Fort Robinson. Although he had surrendered, he remained a hero. Most American Indians, along with a number of white soldiers, admired him.

This made some of the other American Indian leaders there jealous. They did not want the whites to favor Crazy Horse. So, they started a dangerous rumor about him. They said that Crazy Horse planned to run away and fight again. This was not true, but the white people believed it.

No Water had never forgiven Crazy Horse for running off with his wife. Now, he had one of his friends tell General Crook that Crazy Horse was plotting to kill him.

Crook ordered Crazy Horse's arrest. But Crazy Horse had already fled. He and his wife went to her uncle's reservation. They hoped to stay there for a time.

General Crook offered a reward for Crazy Horse's capture. A number of American Indians went after him. Among them were Red Cloud and No Water.

Crazy Horse was anxious to tell General Crook and his men the truth. A white officer at his wife's uncle's reservation tried to help. He arranged for Crazy Horse to return to Fort Robinson to explain things. Crazy Horse went back on September 6, 1877. As he entered, his

At one time, Red Cloud had fought alongside Crazy Horse.

friend, He Dog, rushed over to him. He Dog told Crazy Horse, "Watch your step. You're going into a bad place."

Those were important words. General Crook was no longer interested in what Crazy Horse had to say. He wanted Crazy Horse put in the guardhouse as soon as he arrived. From there, he would be sent to a reservation far away. Crook hoped to separate Crazy Horse from his people. That way, the great leader could not stage an uprising.

Crazy Horse never spoke to Crook that day. Instead, four American Indians took the great

Should Crazy Horse Have a Memorial?

A huge sculpture of Crazy Horse is being carved into the Black Hills. When completed, it will be the world's largest monument. It was started in 1948 by the sculptor Korczak Ziolkowski.

Not everyone is happy about the monument. These include some of Crazy Horse's descendants. They argue that Crazy Horse was a simple person. He did not look for glory. They are also against tearing up the earth to build a monument. The descendants stress that this is not the Sioux way. Below is a model with the partially completed monument in the background.

Crazy Horse 1/34 scale model, Korczak, sculptor, © The Crazy Horse Memorial Foundation, Photo: Robb Dewall

Sioux leader to the guardhouse. One of the American Indians was Little Big Man. He had fought alongside Crazy Horse on many raids.

Crazy Horse saw that he had been tricked. He refused to be locked in a tiny cell. Pulling away from his captors, he drew his knife. But Little Big Man grabbed Crazy Horse from behind and held his arms tightly. Crazy Horse could not defend himself. Seconds later, a white soldier stabbed him with a bayonet. Crazy Horse cried out to the American Indians, "Let me go, my friends. You have hurt me enough."

Crazy Horse died soon afterwards. One of the greatest American Indian leaders was gone. Crazy Horse had never signed a treaty with the United States. He kept the dream of freedom alive as long as he could. He will never be forgotten and will always be an important part of American history.

Timeline

1841—The likely year of Crazy Horse's birth.

1862—Crazy Horse takes part in a raid against the Crow Indians. When he returns, the woman he loves, Black Buffalo Woman, has married another man.

1865—Crazy Horse leads the 11th Cavalry into an ambush over the Platte Bridge Station. The tribal elders make him a "shirt-wearer."

1868—Crazy Horse and others set fire to the abandoned Fort Phil Kearny.

1871—Crazy Horse runs away with Black Buffalo Woman. Her husband, No Water, shoots Crazy Horse but he survives.

1872—Crazy Horse marries a woman named Black Shawl.

1873—Crazy Horse joins with Sitting Bull to conduct a series of attacks on the Northern Pacific Railroad surveying crew.

1875—The government declares that all Sioux must move to a reservation by January 31, 1876.

1876—The Battle of the Little Bighorn is fought on June 25. It is a tremendous American Indian victory. In December, Colonel Nelson Miles fails to get Crazy Horse to surrender.

1877—Crazy Horse surrenders at Fort Robinson in May. On September 6, Crazy Horse is killed by a soldier.

Words to Know

ambush—To hide and then attack.

band—A group of people who are together for a purpose.

bayonet—A long knife fastened to the end of a rifle.

Bozeman Trail—A trail leading to Montana's gold fields that ran through the Sioux's hunting grounds.

cholera—A disease the white people brought into American Indian territory.

decoy—Someone or something that draws another into a trap.

descendant—The relative of someone who died many years before.

elder—An older person with a respected position.

fast—Not eating for a period of time.

game—Wild animals that are hunted for sport or food.

guardhouse—A military jail.

land surveyor—Someone who maps an area of land.

logger—Someone who cuts down trees for a living.

reservation—An area of land set aside for the American Indians by the government.

slaughter—The brutal killing of a large number of individuals.

treaty—A formal agreement between two or more nations.

Reading About Crazy Horse

Anderson, Paul Christopher. *George Armstrong Custer: The Indian Wars and the Battle of the Little Bighorn*. New York: Powerkids Press, 2004.

Birchfield, D. L. *Crazy Horse*. Austin, Tex.: Raintree/Steck Vaughn, January 2003.

Bruhac, Joseph. *Crazy Horse's Vision*. New York: Lee & Low Books, 2000.

George, Charles. *The Sioux*. Farmington Hills, Minnesota: Kidhaven, 2004.

Isaacs, Sally Senzell. *Life in a Sioux Village*. Chicago, Ill.: Heinemann Library, 2000.

Mascoutz, Hal. *George Custer*. Broomall, Penn.: Chelsea House, 2001.

Santella, Andrew. *The Lakota Sioux*. Danbury, Conn.: Children's Press, 2001.

Stein, Conrad R. *The Battle of the Little Bighorn*. Danbury, Conn.: Children's Press, 1997.

Todd, Anne M. *The Sioux: People of the Great Plains*. Mankato, Minn.: Bridgestone Books, 2002.

Internet Addresses

The Battle of the Little Bighorn—Little Bighorn Battlefield

Learn more about one of the Sioux's greatest victories.

<http://www.nps.gov/libi/battle.html>

Travel the Bozeman Trail

Read about the last Western gold rush trail that crossed the Sioux's best hunting grounds.

<http://www.bozemantrail.org>

Index